STUDENT'S
BIBLE
ATLAS

American Map Corporation

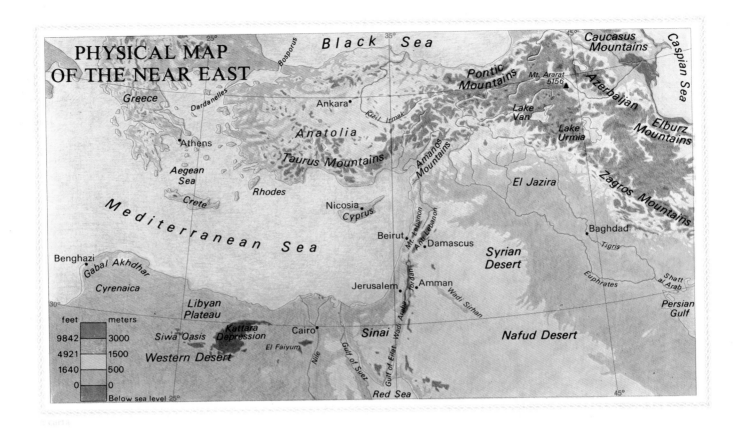

TABLE OF CONTENTS

✱ The ornamental frames are based on ancient motifs.

Published in the Holy Land
by

American Map Corporation

ISBN: 8416-9559-8
Printed in Israel
©Carta

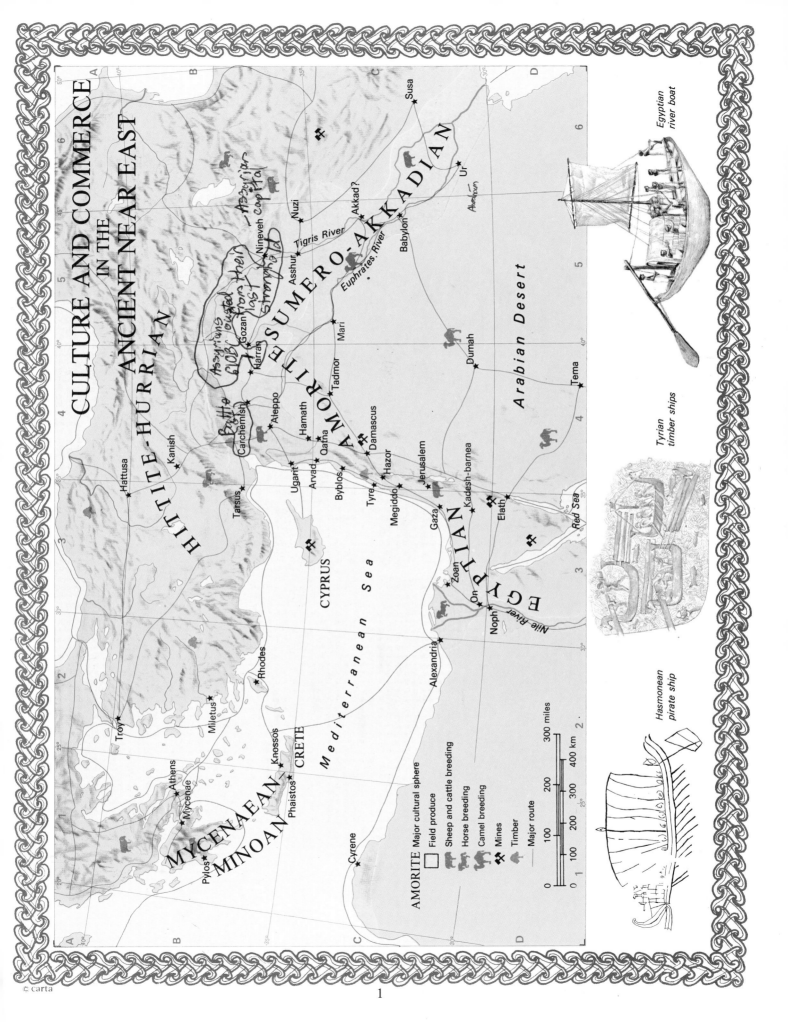

CULTURE AND COMMERCE
IN THE
ANCIENT NEAR EAST

HITTITE-HURRIAN

SUMERO-AKKADIAN

AMORITE

EGYPTIAN

MYCENAEAN-
MINOAN

Arabian Desert

Mediterranean Sea

CYPRUS

CRETE

Red Sea

Nile River

Euphrates River

Tigris River

Susa

Ur
Akkad?
Akkadian

Nuzi
Asshur
Nineveh — Assyrian Capital
Harran
Gozan from their

Assyrians 612 ousted
Brute strength lost

Babylon
Mari
Dumah
Tema

Carchemish
Aleppo
Hamath
Qatna
Tadmor
Damascus
Hazor
Jerusalem
Kadesh-barnea
Elath

Ugarit
Arvad
Byblos
Tyre
Megiddo
Gaza
Zoan
On
Noph

Hattusa
Kanish
Tarsus

Troy
Miletus
Athens
Mycenae
Pylos
Rhodes
Knossos
Phaistos
Cyrene

Alexandria

AMORITE Major cultural sphere
▢ Field produce
🐄 Sheep and cattle breeding
🐎 Horse breeding
🐫 Camel breeding
⚒ Mines
🌲 Timber
— Major route

300 miles
400 km
300
200
100
0

Egyptian river boat

Tyrian timber ships

Hasmonean pirate ship

© carta

1

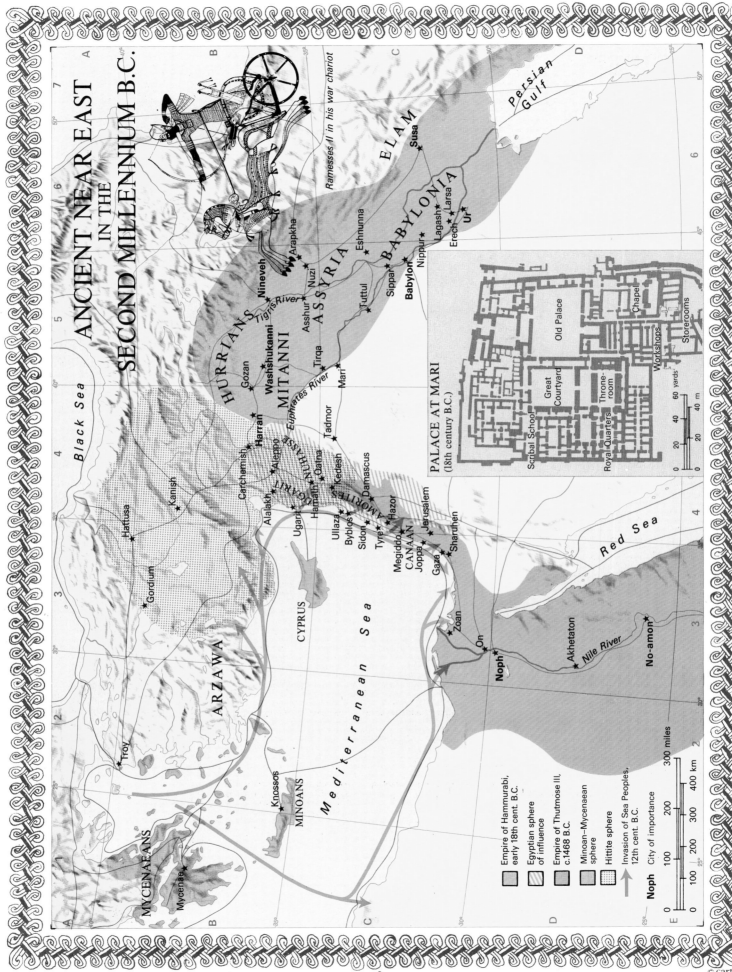

ANCIENT NEAR EAST
IN THE
SECOND MILLENNIUM B.C.

Ramesses II in his war chariot

Black Sea

Persian Gulf

ELAM

Susa

BABYLONIA

Larsa
Lagash
Ur
Erech
Nippur
Sippar
Babylon
Eshnunna
Tuttul

ASSYRIA

Nineveh
Arapkha
Asshur
Nuzi
Tigris River

HURRIANS

Gozan
Washshukanni
MITANNI
Tirqa
Mari
Euphrates River

Harran

Tadmor

Carchemish
Aleppo
NUHASSE
Kanish
Hattusa
Gordium

Alalakh
Ugarit
UGARIT
Hamath
Qatna
Kedesh
Damascus
AMORITES
Hazor
Ullaza
Byblos
Sidon
Tyre
Megiddo
CANAAN
Joppa
Jerusalem
Gaza
Sharuhen

ARZAWA

Troy

CYPRUS

Knossos
MINOANS

MYCENAEANS
Mycenae

Mediterranean Sea

Red Sea

Zoan
On
Noph
Akhetaton
Nile River
No-amon

PALACE AT MARI
(18th century B.C.)

Scribal School
Great Courtyard
Old Palace
Chapel
Throne-room
Royal Quarters
Workshops
Storerooms

60 yards
60 m
40
40
20
20
0

300 miles
400 km
100   200   300   400
0   100   200   300

Empire of Hammurabi, early 18th cent. B.C.
Egyptian sphere of influence
Empire of Thutmose III, c.1468 B.C.
Minoan–Mycenaean sphere
Hittite sphere
Invasion of Sea Peoples, 12th cent. B.C.
Noph City of importance

2

© carta

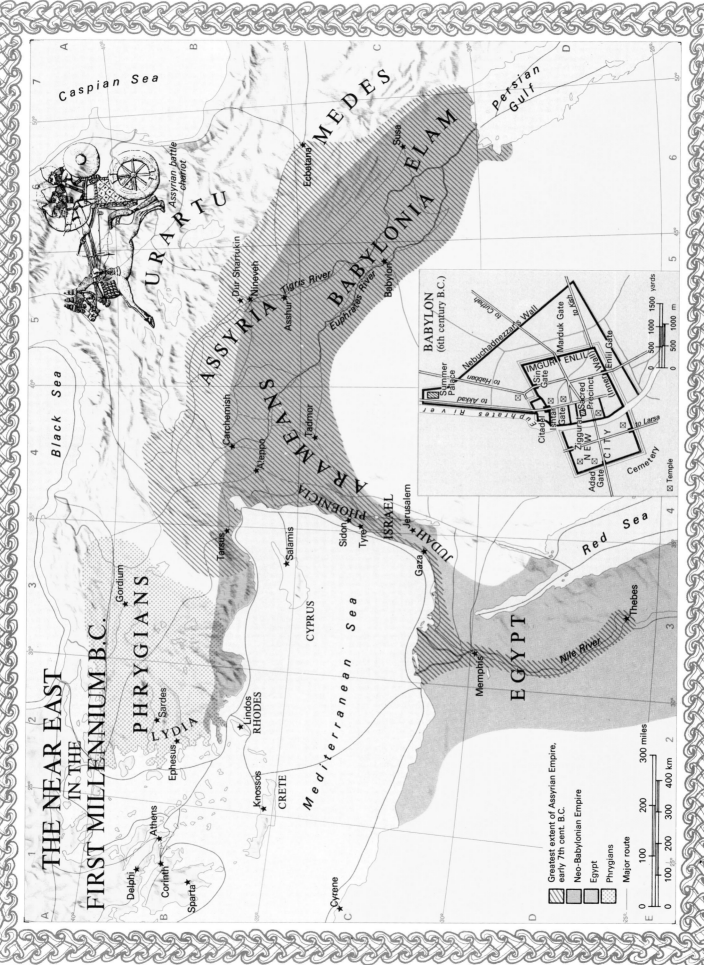

THE NEAR EAST
IN THE
FIRST MILLENNIUM B.C.

Caspian Sea

Black Sea

PHRYGIANS

Gordium

Sardes
LYDIA
Ephesus

Lindos
RHODES

Delphi
Corinth
Athens
Sparta

Knossos
CRETE

Mediterranean Sea

Cyrene

CYPRUS

Salamis

Tarsus

Sidon
Tyre

PHOENICIA
ISRAEL
Jerusalem
JUDAH
Gaza

Memphis

EGYPT

Nile River

Red Sea

Thebes

URARTU

Assyrian battle chariot

MEDES

Ecbatana

Susa

ELAM

Persian Gulf

Dur Sharrukin
Nineveh
Asshur
ASSYRIA

Tigris River

BABYLONIA

Euphrates River

Babylon

ARAMEANS

Carchemish
Aleppo
Tadmor

BABYLON
(6th century B.C.)

Summer Palace
to Akkad
Citadel
Ishtar Gate
Adad Gate

NEW CITY
Ziggurat
Sacred Precinct
Nabu
to Larsa
Cemetery

to Habban
Sin Gate
IMGUR ENLIL
Enlil Gate
Marduk Gate
to Kish
to Cuthah

Nebuchadnezzar's Wall
(Inner Wall)

Euphrates River

⊠ Temple

1500 yards
1000 m
1000
500
500
0

Greatest extent of Assyrian Empire, early 7th cent. B.C.
Neo-Babylonian Empire
Egypt
Phrygians
Major route

0   100   200   300 miles
0   100   200   300   400 km

© carta

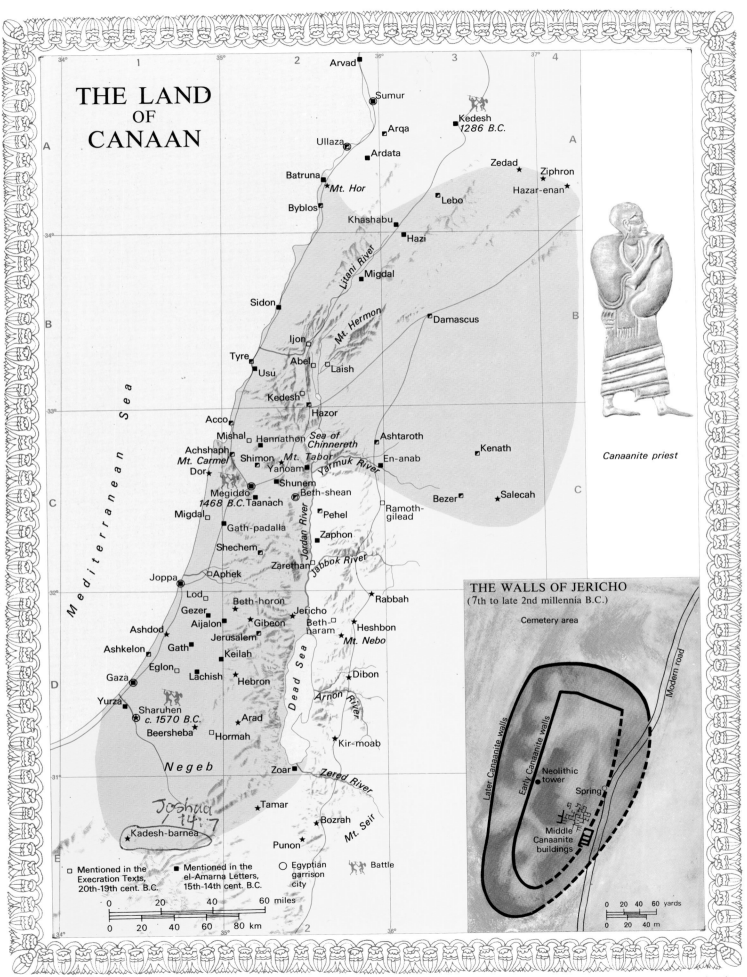

THE LAND OF CANAAN

Arvad

Sumur

Arqa

Kedesh
1286 B.C.

Ullaza

Ardata

Zedad

Ziphron

Batruna

Hazar-enan

Mt. Hor

Byblos

Lebo

Khashabu

Hazi

Litani River

Migdal

Damascus

Sidon

Mt. Hermon

Ijon

Tyre

Abel

Laish

Usu

Kedesh

Ashtaroth

Acco

Hazor

Mishal

Hannathon

Sea of Chinnereth

Achshaph

Kenath

Mt. Carmel

Shimon

Mt. Tabor

En-anab

Dor

Yanoam

Yarmuk River

Shunem

Megiddo
1468 B.C.

Beth-shean

Bezer

Salecah

Taanach

Migdal

Pehel

Ramoth-gilead

Gath-padalla

Zaphon

Shechem

Jordan River

Zarethan

Jabbok River

Joppa

Aphek

Lod

Rabbah

Beth-horon

Gezer

Jericho

Beth-haram

Heshbon

Aijalon

Gibeon

Ashdod

Jerusalem

Keilah

Mt. Nebo

Ashkelon

Gath

Eglon

Lachish

Gaza

Hebron

Dibon

Yurza

Arnon River

Sharuhen
c. 1570 B.C.

Arad

Beersheba

Kir-moab

Hormah

Negeb

Zoar

Zered River

Joshua 14:7

Tamar

Kadesh-barnea

Bozrah

Mt. Seir

Punon

Mediterranean Sea

Dead Sea

Canaanite priest

□ Mentioned in the Execration Texts, 20th–19th cent. B.C.

■ Mentioned in the el-Amarna Letters, 15th–14th cent. B.C.

○ Egyptian garrison city

Battle

| 0 | 20 | 40 | 60 miles |
| 0 | 20 | 40 | 60 | 80 km |

THE WALLS OF JERICHO
(7th to late 2nd millennia B.C.)

Cemetery area

Later Canaanite walls

Early Canaanite walls

Modern road

Neolithic tower

Spring

Middle Canaanite buildings

| 0 | 20 | 40 | 60 yards |
| 0 | 20 | 40 m |

4

© carta

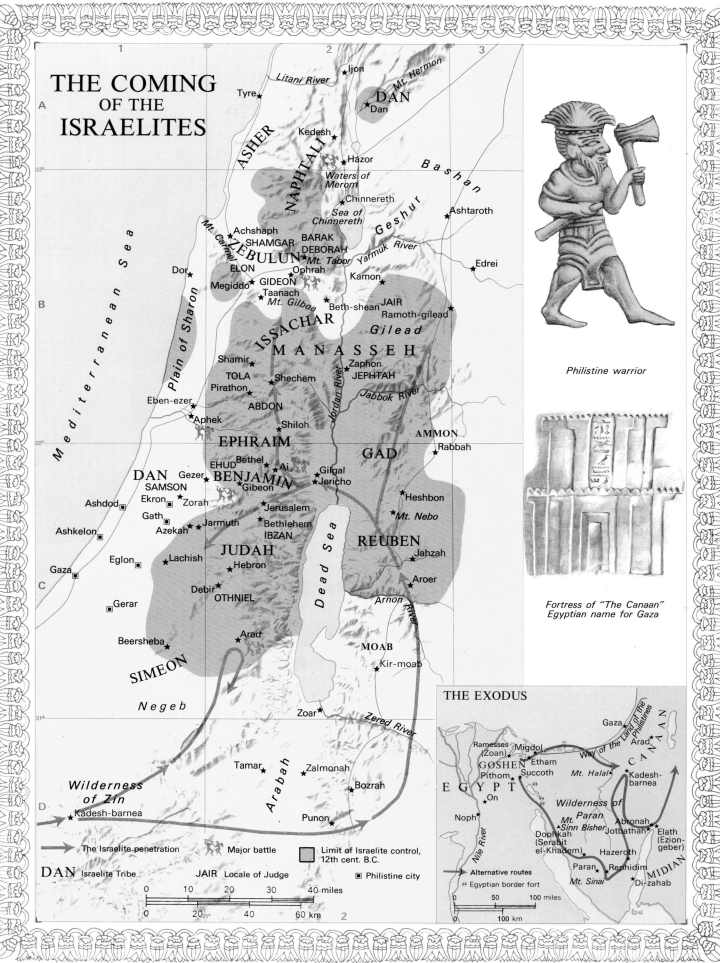

THE COMING OF THE ISRAELITES

A

Litani River
Ijon
Tyre ★
★ Dan
DAN
Mt. Hermon

ASHER
Kedesh ★
NAPHTALI
★ Hazor
Waters of Merom
Bashan

Chinnereth
★
Ashtaroth ★
Sea of Chinnereth
Geshur

Achshaph ★
BARAK
DEBORAH
★ Edrei
SHAMGAR
Yarmuk River

Mt. Carmel
ZEBULUN
Dor ★
ELON
Ophrah ★
Mt. Tabor
Kamon ★

Plain of Sharon
Megiddo ★
GIDEON
Taanach
Mt. Gilboa
Beth-shean ★
JAIR
Ramoth-gilead ★

B

ISSACHAR
Gilead
M A N A S S E H

Shamir ★
Zaphon ★
TOLA
Shechem ★
JEPHTAH
Pirathon ★
Jordan River
Jabbok River

Mediterranean Sea
Eben-ezer ★
ABDON
Aphek ★
★ Shiloh
AMMON

EPHRAIM
GAD
Rabbah ★

Bethel ★
EHUD
Gezer ★
Ai ★
DAN
BENJAMIN
Gilgal ★
SAMSON
Gibeon ★
Jericho ★
Heshbon ★

Ashdod ■
Ekron ■
★ Zorah
Mt. Nebo ★
Gath ■
Jerusalem ★

C

Ashkelon ■
Azekah ★
Jarmuth ★
Bethlehem ★
IBZAN
REUBEN

Gaza ■
Eglon ■
Lachish ★
JUDAH
Hebron ★
Jahzah ★

Gerar ■
Debir ★
OTHNIEL
Aroer ★

Beersheba ★
Arad ★
Arnon River

SIMEON
Dead Sea
MOAB
Kir-moab ★

Negeb
Zoar ★
Zered River

D

Wilderness of Zin
★ Kadesh-barnea
Arabah
Tamar ★
Zalmonah ★
Bozrah ★
Punon ★

→ The Israelite penetration
Major battle
▨ Limit of Israelite control, 12th cent. B.C.

DAN Israelite Tribe
JAIR Locale of Judge
■ Philistine city

0 10 20 30 40 miles
0 20 40 60 km

Philistine warrior

Fortress of "The Canaan" Egyptian name for Gaza

THE EXODUS

Gaza ★
Ramesses (Zoan) ★
Migdol
Way of the Land of the Philistines
Arad ★
GOSHEN
Etham
Pithom ★
Succoth
Mt. Halal
C A N A A N

E G Y P T
★ On
Kadesh-barnea ★

Nile River
Noph ★
Wilderness of Paran
Abronah ★
Jotbathah ★
Elath (Ezion-geber) ★

Dophkah (Serabit el-Khadem) ★
Mt. Sinn Bisher
Hazeroth ★
MIDIAN

Paran ★
Rephidim ★
Mt. Sinai ★
Di-zahab ★

→ Alternative routes
Egyptian border fort

0 50 100 miles
0 100 km

5

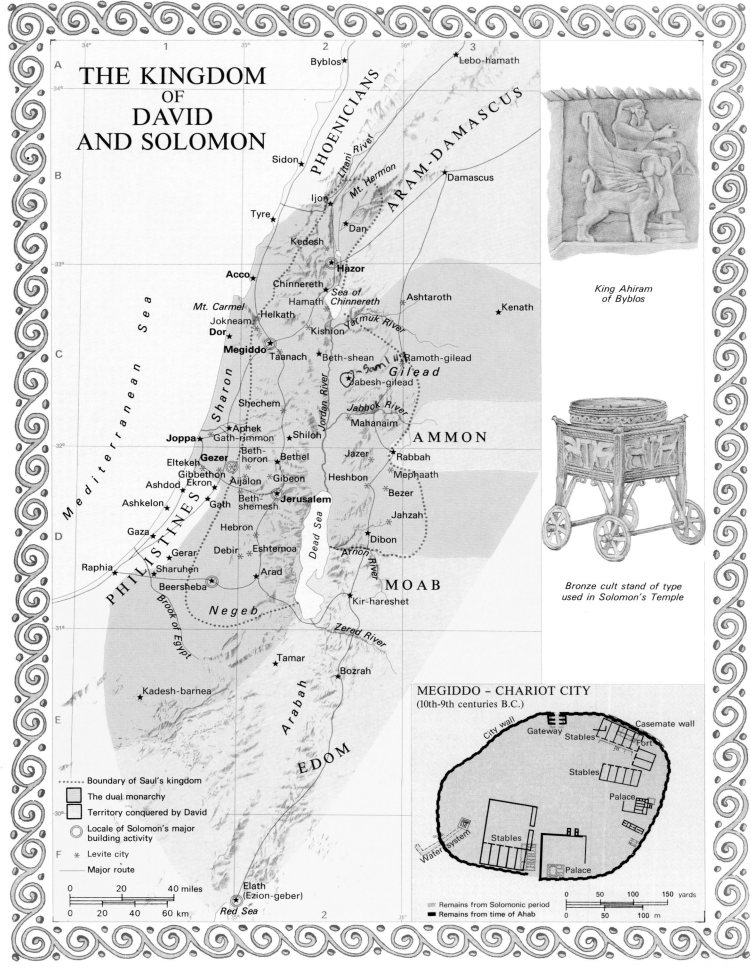

THE KINGDOM OF DAVID AND SOLOMON

A

Byblos ★
Lebo-hamath ★

PHOENICIANS

Sidon ★

ARAM-DAMASCUS

B

Litani River
Mt. Hermon
Ijon ★
Damascus ★
Tyre ★
Dan ★
Kedesh ★

Acco ★
Hazor ★
Chinnereth ★
Sea of Chinnereth
Ashtaroth ✳
Kenath ★
Mt. Carmel
Hamath ★
Helkath ✳
Yarmuk River
Jokneam ✳
Dor ★
Kishion ✳
~ Sam l
Megiddo ⊚
Taanach ✳
Beth-shean ★
Ramoth-gilead ✳
Gilead
Jabesh-gilead ★

C

Sharon
Shechem ★
Jabbok River
Mahanaim ★
Joppa ★
Aphek ★
Gath-rimmon ✳
Shiloh ★
AMMON
Jazer ★
Rabbah ★
Gezer ⊚
Beth-horon ✳
Bethel ★
Eltekeh ✳
Heshbon ★
Mephaath ✳
Gibbethon ✳
Ekron ★
Aijalon ✳
Gibeon ★
Ashdod ★
Bezer ✳
Gath ★
Beth-shemesh ★
Jerusalem ★
Ashkelon ★
Jahzah ✳
Gaza ★
Hebron ★
Dibon ★
Debir ✳
Eshtemoa ✳
Dead Sea
Arnon River
Gerar ★
Raphia ★
Sharuhen ✳
Arad ★
MOAB
Beersheba ★

D

Mediterranean Sea
PHILISTINES

Kir-haresheth ★

Negeb

Zered River

E

Tamar ★
Bozrah ★
Kadesh-barnea ★

Arabah

EDOM

Boundary of Saul's kingdom
The dual monarchy
Territory conquered by David
⊚ Locale of Solomon's major building activity
✳ Levite city
Major route

0   20   40 miles
0   20   40   60 km

Elath ★
(Ezion-geber)
Red Sea

F

King Ahiram of Byblos

Bronze cult stand of type used in Solomon's Temple

MEGIDDO – CHARIOT CITY
(10th-9th centuries B.C.)

City wall
Gateway
Stables
Casemate wall
Fort
Stables
Palace
Water System
Stables
Palace

▨ Remains from Solomonic period
▬ Remains from time of Ahab

0   50   100   150   yards
0   50   100   m

6

© carta

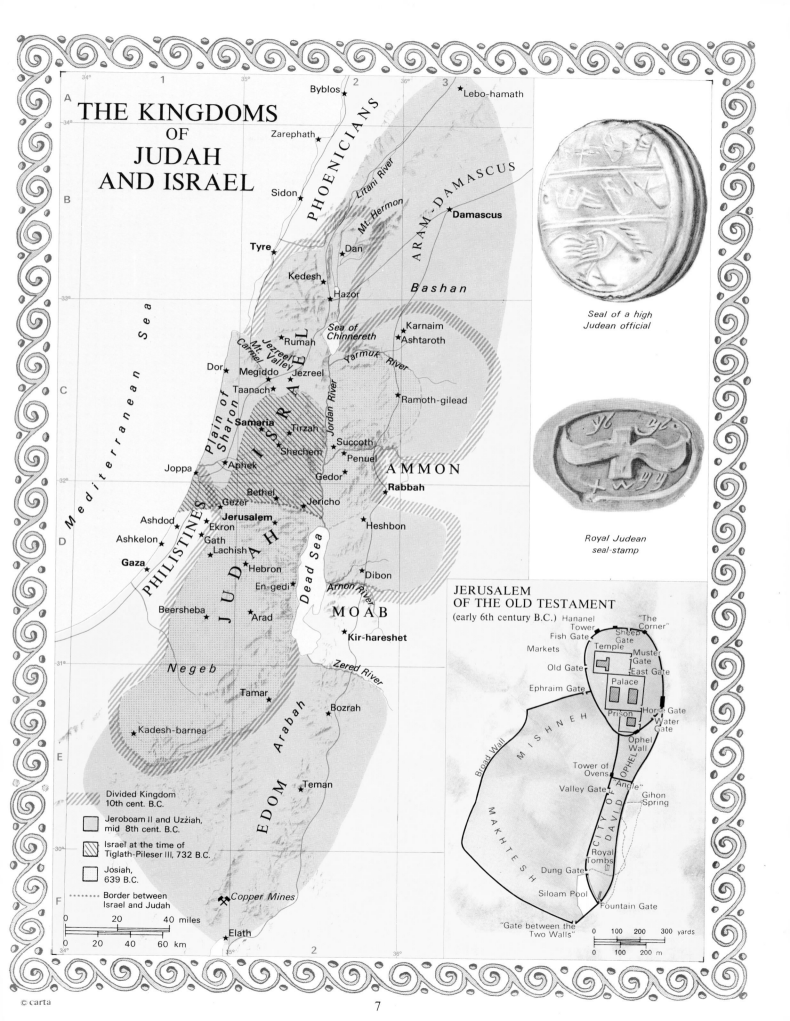

THE KINGDOMS OF JUDAH AND ISRAEL

Byblos
Lebo-hamath

Zarephath

PHOENICIANS
Litani River
ARAM-DAMASCUS

Sidon
Mt. Hermon
Damascus

Tyre
Dan

Kedesh
Hazor
Bashan

Mediterranean Sea

Sea of Chinnereth
Karnaim
Ashtaroth

Rumah
Mt. Carmel
Jezreel Valley
Dor
Megiddo
Jezreel
Yarmuk River

ISRAEL
Taanach
Ramoth-gilead

Plain of Sharon
Samaria
Tirzah
Jordan River

Aphek
Shechem
Succoth

Joppa
Gedor
Penuel

AMMON

Bethel
Jericho
Rabbah

Gezer
Jerusalem
Heshbon

Ashdod
Ekron
PHILISTINES

Ashkelon
Gath
Lachish

Gaza
Hebron
Dead Sea
Dibon

En-gedi
Arnon River

Beersheba
Arad
MOAB

JUDAH

Kir-hareshet

Negeb
Zered River

Tamar
Bozrah

Kadesh-barnea
Arabah

EDOM
Teman

Divided Kingdom
10th cent. B.C.

Jeroboam II and Uzziah,
mid 8th cent. B.C.

Israel at the time of
Tiglath-Pileser III, 732 B.C.

Josiah,
639 B.C.

Border between
Israel and Judah

Copper Mines
Elath

0   20   40 miles
0 20 40 60 km

*Seal of a high
Judean official*

*Royal Judean
seal-stamp*

JERUSALEM OF THE OLD TESTAMENT
(early 6th century B.C.)

Hananel Tower
"The Corner"
Fish Gate
Sheep Gate
Markets
Temple
Muster Gate
Old Gate
East Gate
Ephraim Gate
Palace
Horse Gate
Prison
Water Gate
Broad Wall
Ophel Wall
MISHNEH
Tower of Ovens
"Angle"
Valley Gate
Gihon Spring
CITY OF DAVID
OPHEL
MAKHTESH
Royal Tombs
Dung Gate
Siloam Pool
Fountain Gate
"Gate between the Two Walls"

0 100 200 300 yards
0 100 200 m

© carta

7

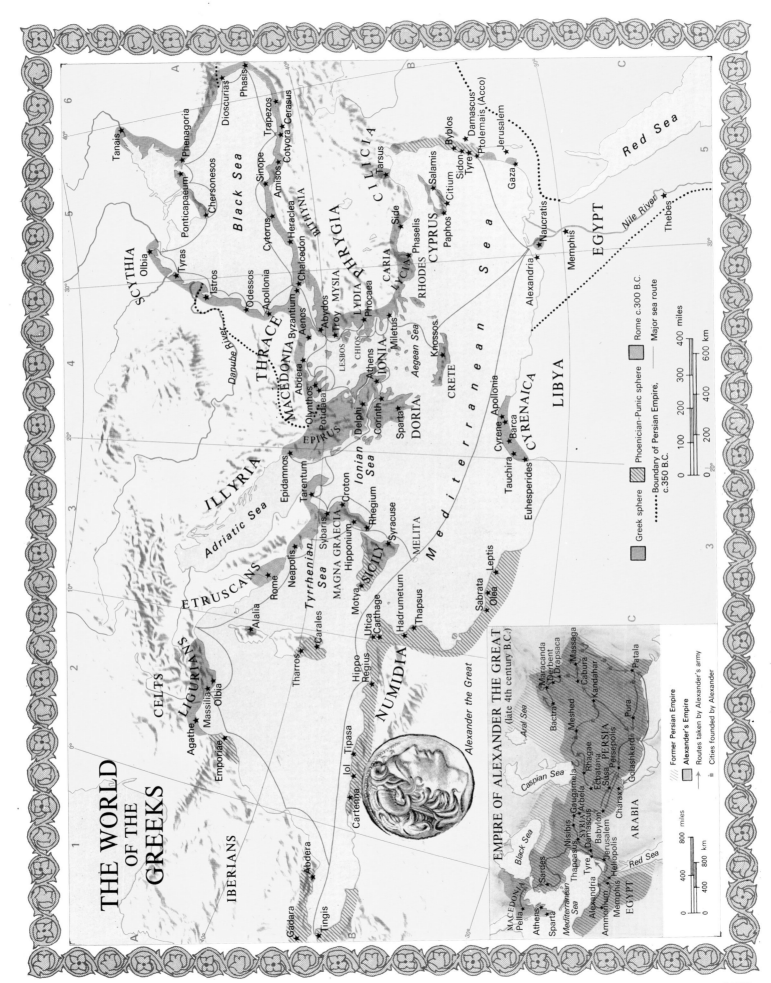

THE WORLD
OF THE
GREEKS

IBERIANS

CELTS

LIGURIA

Emporiae
Agathe
Massilia
Olbia

Alalia

Tharros

Carales

Rome
Neapolis
Tarentum

ETRUSCANS

Tyrrhenian Sea

MAGNA GRAECIA

Croton
Sybaris
Rhegium
Hipponium

SICILY

Syracuse

Motya

Utica
Carthage

Hadrumetum

Thapsus

NUMIDIA

Hippo Regius

Tipasa
Jol
Cartenna

Tingis

Gadara

Abdera

Adriatic Sea

ILLYRIA

Epidamnos

EPIRUS

MACEDONIA
Olynthos
Potidaea

Abdera
Aenos

THRACE

Byzantium

Chalcedon

Danube River

SCYTHIA

Olbia
Tyras

Istros
Odessos
Apollonia

Black Sea

Tyras
Ponticapaeum
Chersonesos

Tanais
Phenagoria

Dioscurias
Phasis

Trapezos
Cerasus
Cotyora
Amisos
Sinope
Cytorus
Heraclea

BITHYNIA

MYSIA
Troy
Abydos
Phocaea

PHRYGIA

LYDIA
IONIA
Miletus

CARIA

LESBOS
CHIOS

DORIA

Delphi
Athens
Corinth
Sparta

Ionian Sea

Aegean Sea

Knossos

CRETE

LYCIA
Side
Phaselis

RHODES

CILICIA
Tarsus

Salamis
Citium
Paphos

CYPRUS

Byblos
Sidon
Tyre

Damascus
Ptolemais (Acco)
Jerusalem

Gaza

Naucratis

Alexandria

Memphis

EGYPT

Nile River

Thebes

Red Sea

Mediterranean Sea

LIBYA

CYRENAICA
Apollonia
Cyrene
Barca

Tauchira
Euhesperides

Leptis
Sabrata
Oea

Thapsus

MELITA

Legend

Greek sphere	Rome c. 300 B.C.
Phoenician-Punic sphere	Major sea route
Boundary of Persian Empire, c.350 B.C.	

0 100 200 300 400 miles
0 200 400 600 km

EMPIRE OF ALEXANDER THE GREAT
(late 4th century B.C.)

MACEDONIA
Pella
Athens
Sparta

Black Sea

Sardes

Mediterranean Sea

Alexandria
Ammonium
Memphis
Heliopolis

EGYPT

Red Sea

Thapsacus
Nisibis
Damascus
Tyre
Jerusalem

SYRIA

Babylon
Charax

ARABIA

Caspian Sea
Aral Sea

Bactra
Maracanda
Derbent
Drapsaca
Massaga
Cabura
Kandahar

Meshed

Rhagae
Ecbatana
Susa
PERSIA
Persepolis
Pura
Golashkerd
Patala

Gaugamela
Arbela

Former Persian Empire	
Alexander's Empire	
→	Routes taken by Alexander's army
⚓	Cities founded by Alexander

0 400 800 miles
0 400 800 km

Alexander the Great

© carta

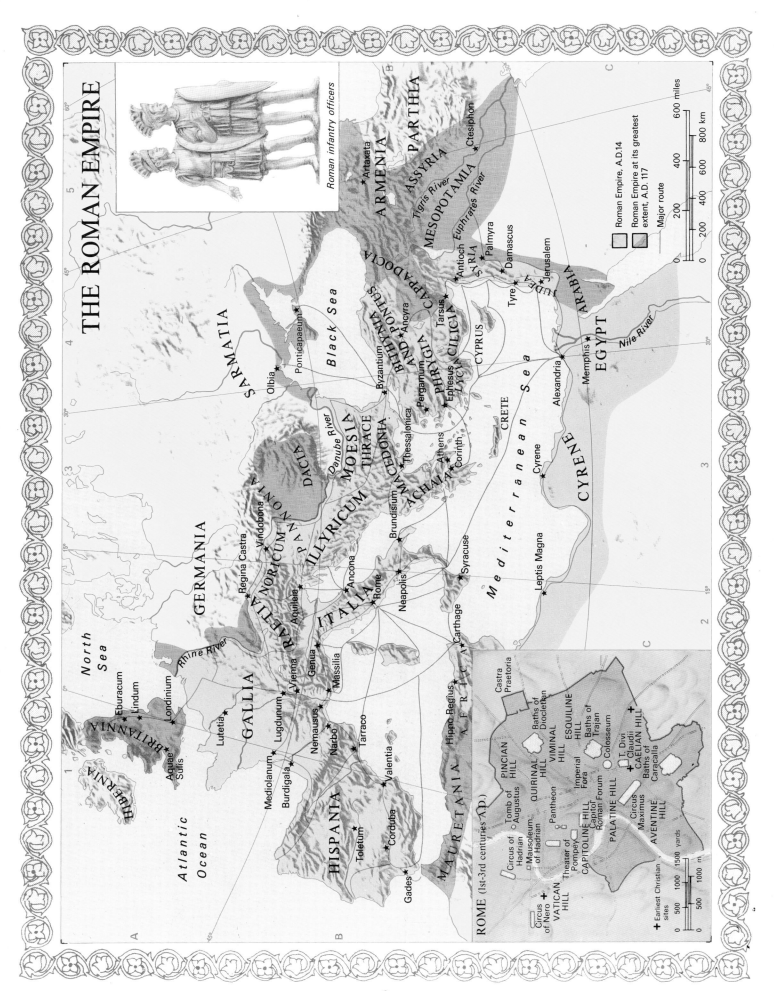

THE ROMAN EMPIRE

Roman infantry officers

Roman Empire, A.D.14
Roman Empire at its greatest extent, A.D. 117
Major route

600 miles
800 km
400
600
400
200
200
0
0

Inset — labels on main map

ARMENIA · Artaxata
PARTHIA
ASSYRIA
MESOPOTAMIA
Tigris River
Euphrates River · Ctesiphon
Antioch · Palmyra
SYRIA · Damascus
Tyre
Jerusalem
JUDEA
ARABIA
EGYPT
Memphis
Alexandria
Nile River

CAPPADOCIA
BITHYNIA
PONTUS
Ancyra
Tarsus
CILICIA
PHRYGIA
LYCIA
Pergamum
Ephesus
CYPRUS
CRETE

SARMATIA
Ponticapaeum
Olbia
Black Sea
Byzantium
PANNONIA
DACIA
Danube River
MOESIA
THRACE
MACEDONIA
Thessalonica
Athens
Corinth
ACHAIA
Mediterranean Sea
Cyrene
CYRENE
Leptis Magna

GERMANIA
Regina Castra
Vindobona
NORICUM
RAETIA
Aquileia
ITALIA
Ancona
Rome
Neapolis
Brundisium
Syracuse
Carthage
AFRICA
Hippo Regius
MAURETANIA
ILLYRICUM

North Sea
Atlantic Ocean
BRITANNIA
HIBERNIA
Eburacum
Lindum
Londinium
Aquae Sulis
GALLIA
Lutetia
Lugdunum
Burdigala
Nemausus
Narbo
Vienna
Genua
Massilia
Mediolanum
HISPANIA
Toletum
Corduba
Gades
Valentia
Tarraco

ROME (1st–3rd centuries A.D.)

Castra Praetoria
Baths of Diocletian
PINCIAN HILL
Tomb of Augustus
Circus of Hadrian
VATICAN HILL
Circus of Nero
Mausoleum of Hadrian
QUIRINAL HILL
VIMINAL HILL
ESQUILINE HILL
Baths of Trajan
Colosseum
Pantheon
Imperial Fora
Roman Forum
CAPITOLINE HILL
Capitol
Theater of Pompey
PALATINE HILL
Circus Maximus
CAELIAN HILL
T. Divi Claudii
Baths of Caracalla
AVENTINE HILL

Earliest Christian sites

1500 yards
1000 m
1000
500
500
0
0

9

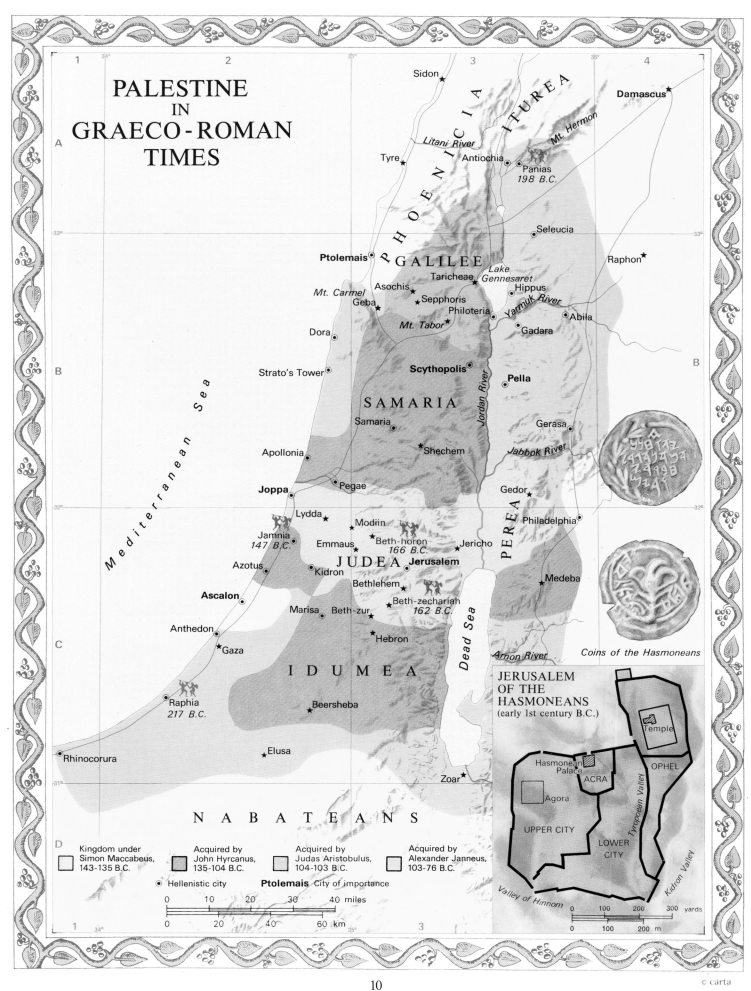

PALESTINE IN GRAECO-ROMAN TIMES

Mediterranean Sea

Sidon

PHOENICIA
ITUREA

Damascus

Litani River

Mt. Hermon

Tyre
Antiochia
Panias
198 B.C.

Seleucia

Raphon

Ptolemais
GALILEE

Taricheae
Lake Gennesaret
Hippus

Asochis
Mt. Carmel
Geba
Sepphoris
Philoteria
Yarmuk River
Abila

Dora
Mt. Tabor
Gadara

Strato's Tower

SAMARIA

Scythopolis
Pella
Jordan River

Samaria
Gerasa

Shechem
Jabbok River

Apollonia

Joppa
Pegae
Gedor
Philadelphia
PEREA

Lydda
Modiin

Jamnia
147 B.C.
Emmaus
Beth-horon
166 B.C.
Jericho

Azotus
JUDEA
Jerusalem

Kidron
Bethlehem
Medeba

Ascalon
Beth-zechariah
162 B.C.

Marisa
Beth-zur

Anthedon
Hebron

Gaza
Dead Sea

IDUMEA

Raphia
217 B.C.
Beersheba
Arnon River

Elusa

Zoar

Rhinocorura

NABATEANS

Coins of the Hasmoneans

JERUSALEM OF THE HASMONEANS
(early 1st century B.C.)

Temple
Hasmonean Palace
OPHEL
ACRA
Tyropoeon Valley
Agora
UPPER CITY
LOWER CITY
Valley of Hinnom
Kidron Valley

0   100   200   300 yards
0   100   200 m

Kingdom under Simon Maccabeus, 143-135 B.C.	Acquired by John Hyrcanus, 135-104 B.C.	Acquired by Judas Aristobulus, 104-103 B.C.	Acquired by Alexander Janneus, 103-76 B.C.

⊙ Hellenistic city   **Ptolemais** City of importance

0   10   20   30   40 miles
0   20   40   60 km

© carta

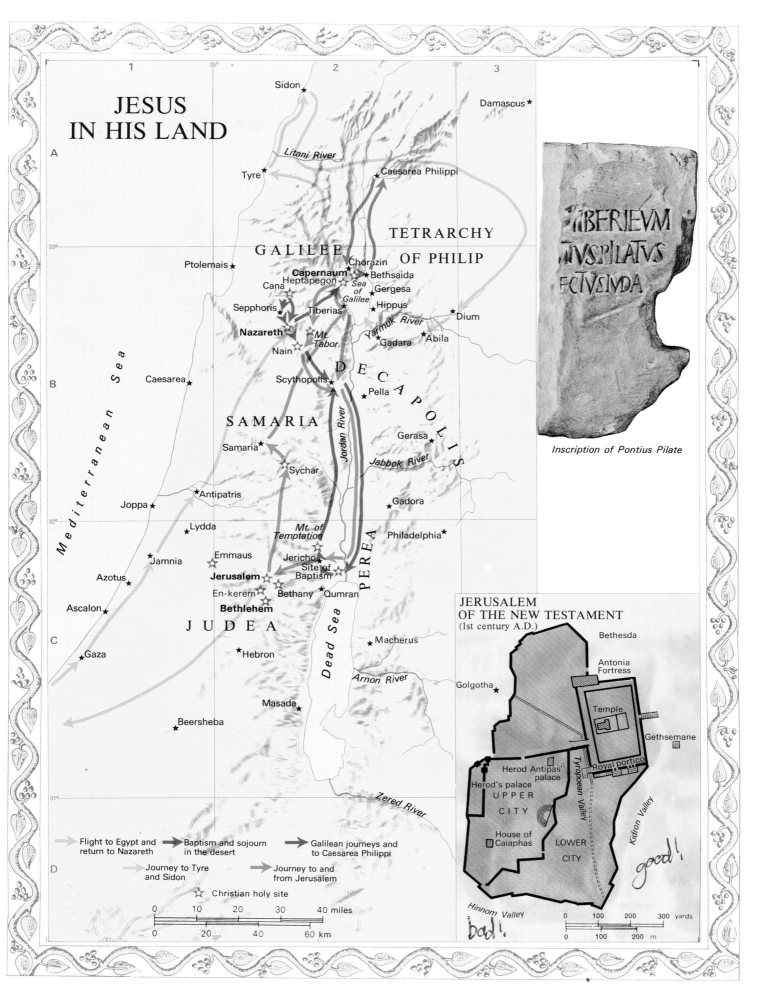

JESUS
IN HIS LAND

Sidon

Damascus

Litani River

TETRARCHY

GALILEE   Chorazin   OF PHILIP

Tyre

Caesarea Philippi

Ptolemais

Capernaum   Bethsaida
Heptapegon   *Sea*
Cana   *of*   Gergesa
Galilee
Sepphoris   Tiberias   Hippus

Nazareth   *Mt.*   Dium
Tabor
Nain   *Yarmuk River*
Gadara   Abila

D E C A P O L I S

Caesarea

Scythopolis   Pella

S A M A R I A   *Jordan River*

Samaria   Gerasa

Sychar   *Jabbok River*

Antipatris

Joppa   Gadora

Lydda   *Mt. of*   Philadelphia
Temptation
Emmaus   Jericho   P E R E A
Jamnia
Jerusalem   Site of
Baptism
Azotus   En-kerem   Bethany   Qumran
Bethlehem
Ascalon   J U D E A
Dead Sea
Gaza   Hebron   Macherus

Arnon River

Masada

Beersheba

Mediterranean Sea

Zered River

Inscription of Pontius Pilate

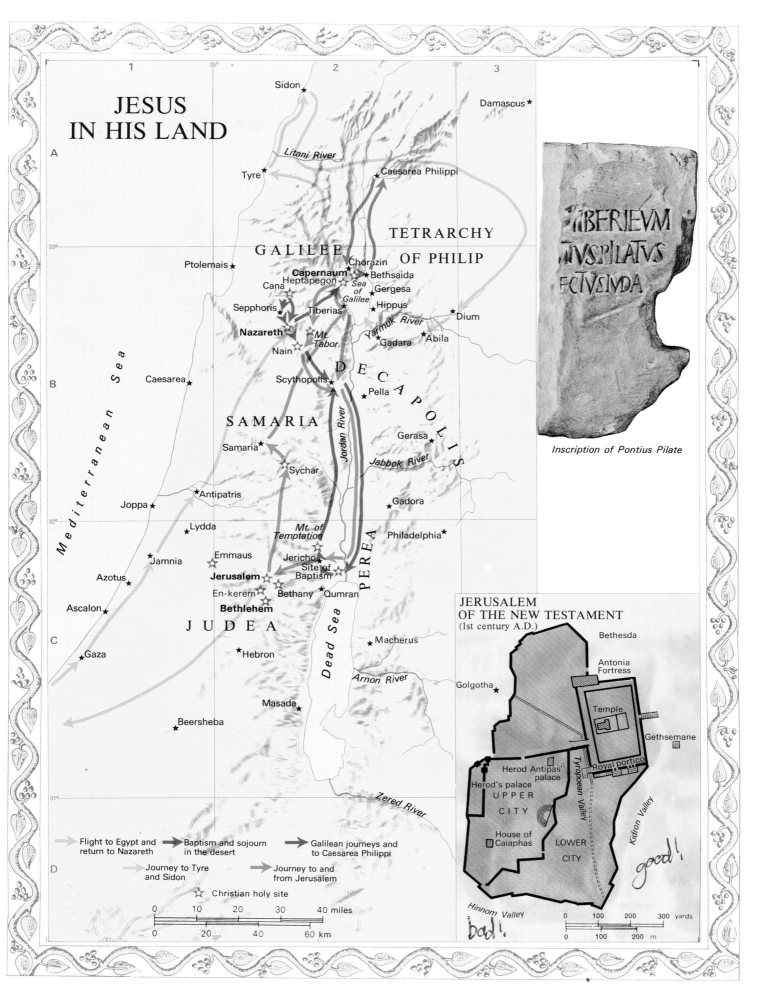

JERUSALEM
OF THE NEW TESTAMENT
(1st century A.D.)

Bethesda

Golgotha   Antonia
Fortress

Temple

Gethsemane

Royal portico

Herod Antipas'
palace

Herod's palace   UPPER
CITY   *Tyropoean Valley*

House of
Caiaphas   LOWER
CITY   *Kidron Valley*

Hinnom Valley

→ Flight to Egypt and   → Baptism and sojourn   → Galilean journeys and
return to Nazareth   in the desert   to Caesarea Philippi

→ Journey to Tyre   → Journey to and
and Sidon   from Jerusalem

☆ Christian holy site

0   10   20   30   40 miles

0   20   40   60 km

0   100   200   300 yards

0   100   200 m

© carta

11

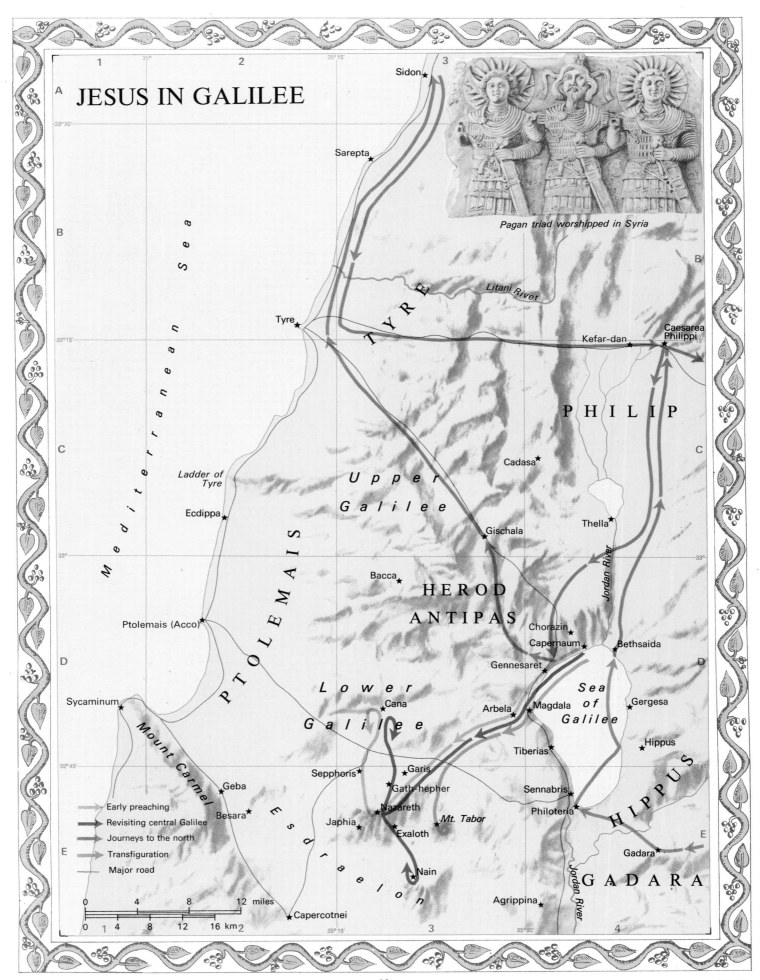

JESUS IN GALILEE

Pagan triad worshipped in Syria

Sidon

Sarepta

Mediterranean Sea

TYRE

Litani River

Tyre

Caesarea Philippi

Kefar-dan

PHILIP

Ladder of Tyre

Cadasa

Upper Galilee

Ecdippa

Gischala

Thella

Jordan River

Bacca

HEROD ANTIPAS

Ptolemais (Acco)

PTOLEMAIS

Chorazin

Capernaum

Bethsaida

Gennesaret

Lower Galilee

Cana

Sea of Galilee

Sycaminum

Arbela

Magdala

Gergesa

Hippus

Tiberias

Mount Carmel

Sepphoris

Garis

Geba

Gath-hepher

Sennabris

Besara

Nazareth

Philoteria

HIPPUS

Japhia

Mt. Tabor

Exaloth

Esdraelon

Gadara

Nain

Agrippina

Jordan River

GADARA

Early preaching
Revisiting central Galilee
Journeys to the north
Transfiguration
Major road

0   4   8   12 miles
0 1 4   8   12   16 km

Capercotnei

12

c carta

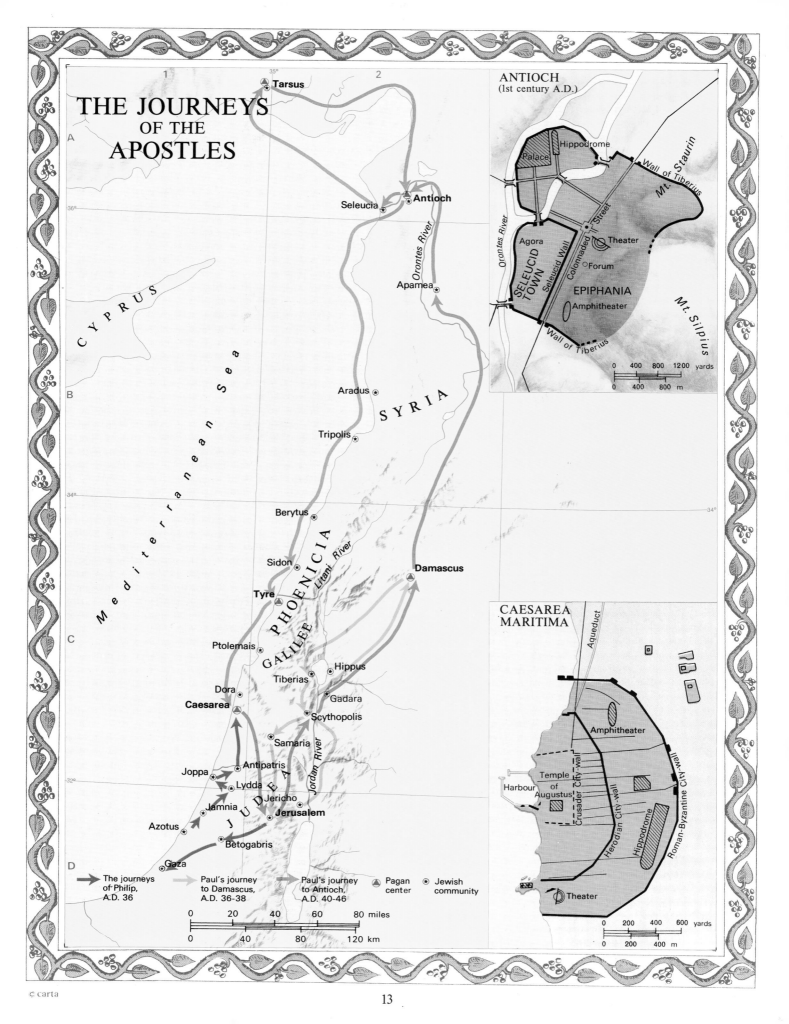

THE JOURNEYS
OF THE
APOSTLES

Tarsus

Antioch
Seleucia

Apamea
Orontes River

C Y P R U S

Mediterranean Sea

Aradus

S Y R I A

Tripolis

Berytus

Sidon
Litani River

PHOENICIA

Tyre

Damascus

GALILEE

Ptolemais

Hippus
Tiberias

Dora
Gadara

Caesarea
Scythopolis

Samaria

Joppa
Antipatris
Jordan River

Lydda
Jericho

Jamnia
J U D E A
Jerusalem

Azotus

Betogabris

Gaza

The journeys of Philip, A.D. 36

Paul's journey to Damascus, A.D. 36-38

Paul's journey to Antioch, A.D. 40-46

Pagan center

Jewish community

| 0 | 20 | 40 | 60 | 80 miles |
| 0 | 40 | 80 | 120 km |

ANTIOCH
(1st century A.D.)

Palace
Hippodrome

Orontes River

Agora
Seleucid Wall

SELEUCID
TOWN

EPIPHANIA

Colonnaded Street

Theater

Forum

Amphitheater

Mt. Staurin

Mt. Silpius

Wall of Tiberius

| 0 | 400 | 800 | 1200 | yards |
| 0 | 400 | 800 | m |

CAESAREA
MARITIMA

Aqueduct

Amphitheater

Harbour

Temple of Augustus

Crusader City-wall

Herodian City-wall

Hippodrome

Roman-Byzantine City-wall

Theater

| 0 | 200 | 400 | 600 | yards |
| 0 | 200 | 400 | m |

© carta

13

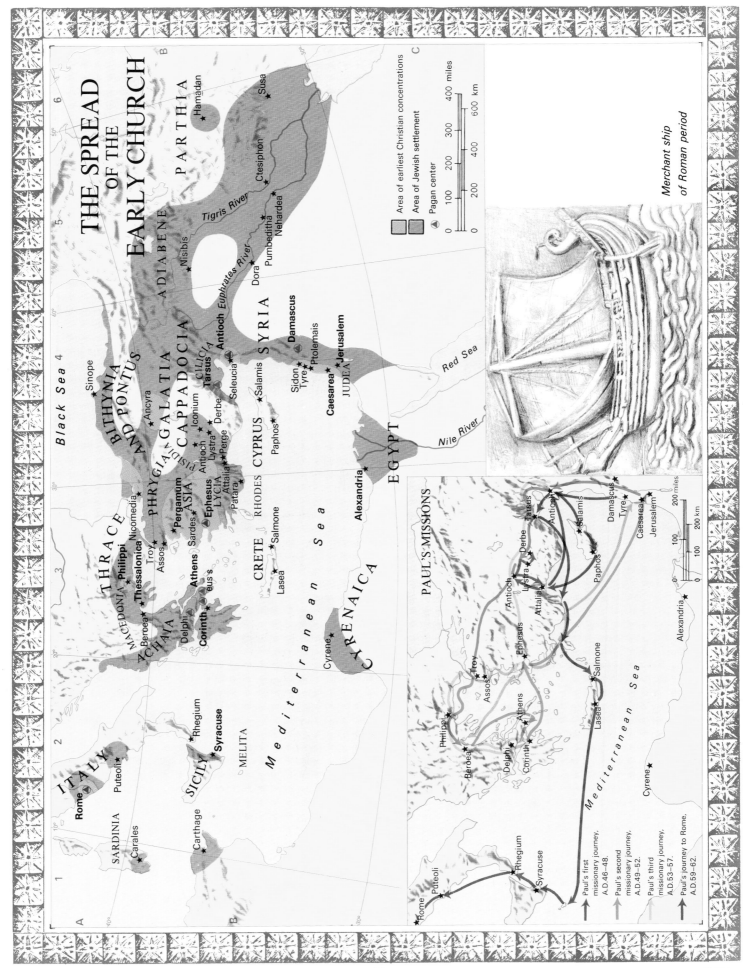

THE SPREAD OF THE EARLY CHURCH

PARTHIA

★ Susa
★ Hamadan

ADIABENE

Tigris River
★ Ctesiphon
★ Nisibis
★ Pumbeditha
★ Nehardea

Euphrates River

★ Dora

SYRIA

Antioch
★ Tarsus
Damascus

CILICIA
★ Seleucia
★ Salamis
★ Sidon
★ Tyre
★ Ptolemais
Caesarea
Jerusalem

JUDEA

Black Sea 4

★ Sinope

BITHYNIA AND PONTUS

GALATIA
★ Ancyra

CAPPADOCIA

PHRYGIA
★ Iconium
★ Derbe

ASIA
★ Antioch
★ Lystra
★ Perge

PISIDIA

Pergamum
★ Sardes
Ephesus
★ Attalia

LYCIA
★ Patara

THRACE
★ Nicomedia
★ Troy
★ Assos

MACEDONIA
Philippi
Thessalonica
★ Beroea

ACHAIA
★ Delphi
Athens
Corinth
...eus's

CRETE
★ Salmone
★ Lasea

RHODES **CYPRUS**
★ Paphos

EGYPT

Alexandria

Nile River

Red Sea

CYRENAICA
★ Cyrene

Mediterranean Sea

ITALY
Rome
★ Puteoli

SICILY
★ Rhegium
Syracuse

SARDINIA
★ Carales

★ Carthage

MELITA

Legend

Area of earliest Christian concentrations

Area of Jewish settlement

★ Pagan center

| | 100 | 200 | 300 | 400 miles |
| 0 | 200 | 400 | 600 km |

Merchant ship of Roman period

PAUL'S MISSIONS

★ Tarsus
★ Antioch
★ Salamis
★ Damascus
★ Tyre
★ Caesarea
★ Jerusalem
★ Antioch
★ Derbe
★ Lystra
★ Attalia
★ Paphos
★ Ephesus
★ Troy
★ Assos
★ Athens
★ Salmone
★ Lasea
★ Philippi
★ Beroea
★ Delphi
★ Corinth
★ Cyrene
★ Alexandria
★ Puteoli
★ Rhegium
★ Syracuse
★ Rome

Mediterranean Sea

| | 100 | 200 miles |
| 0 | 100 | 200 km |

→ Paul's first missionary journey, A.D. 46–48.

→ Paul's second missionary journey, A.D. 49–52.

→ Paul's third missionary journey, A.D. 53–57.

→ Paul's journey to Rome, A.D. 59–62.

14

© carta

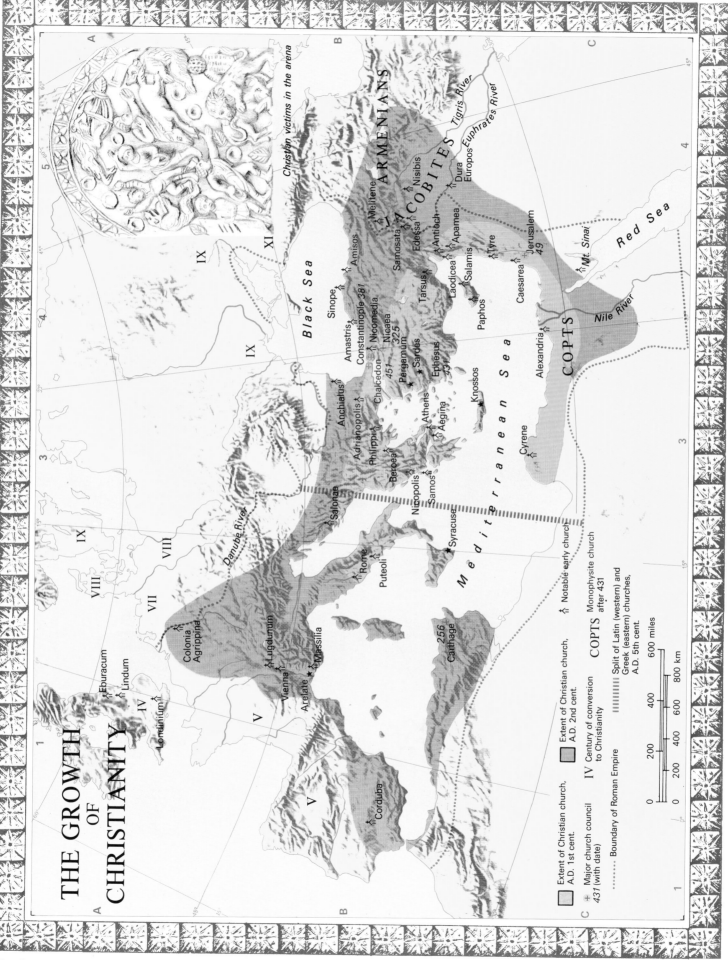

THE GROWTH
OF
CHRISTIANITY

Christian victims in the arena

Legend:

- Extent of Christian church, A.D. 1st cent.
- Major church council 431 (with date)
- Extent of Christian church, A.D. 2nd cent.
- IV Century of conversion to Christianity
- Boundary of Roman Empire
- COPTS Monophysite church after 431
- Notable early church
- Split of Latin (western) and Greek (eastern) churches, A.D. 5th cent.

Scale: 0 200 400 600 miles / 0 200 400 600 800 km

ARMENIANS
JACOBITES
COPTS

Tigris River
Euphrates River
Red Sea
Black Sea
Mediterranean Sea
Danube River
Nile River
Mt. Sinai

Melitene
Nisibis
Samosata
Dura Europos
Edessa
Antioch
Amisos
Sinope
Amastris
Constantinople 381
Nicomedia
Nicaea 325
Chalcedon 451
Pergamum
Sardes
Ephesus 431
Tarsus
Apamea
Laodicea
Salamis
Tyre
Paphos
Caesarea
Jerusalem 49
Alexandria
Cyrene
Knossos
Athens
Aegina
Samos
Nicopolis
Beroea
Philippi
Adrianopolis
Anchialus
Salonae
Syracuse
Rome
Puteoli
Carthage 256
Corduba
Massilia
Arelate
Vienna
Lugdunum
Colonia Agrippina
Eburacum
Lindum
Londinium

© carta

15

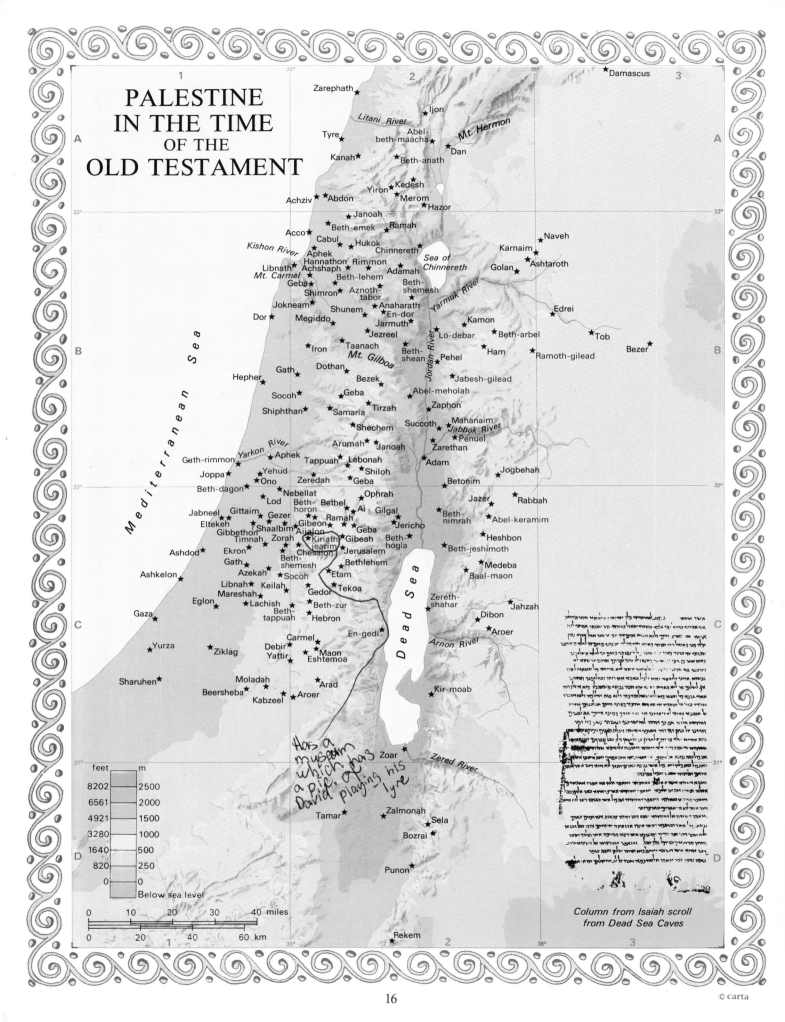

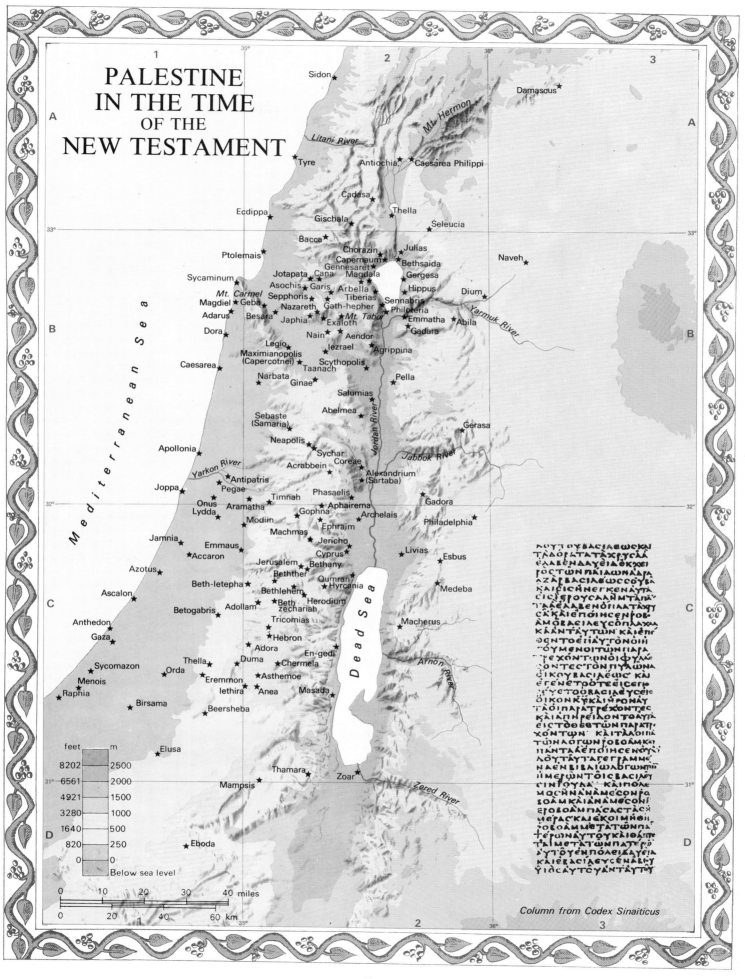

PALESTINE
IN THE TIME
OF THE
NEW TESTAMENT

Mediterranean Sea

Litani River

Mt. Hermon

Sidon

Damascus

Tyre

Antiochia Caesarea Philippi

Cadasa

Ecdippa

Thella

Gischala

Seleucia

Bacca

Ptolemais

Chorazin Julias

Capernaum Bethsaida

Gennesaret Naveh

Jotapata Cana Magdala Gergesa

Sycaminum Asochis Garis Arbella Hippus

Mt. Carmel Sepphoris Tiberias Dium

Magdiel Geba Nazareth Gath-hepher Sennabris

Adarus Besara Japhia Mt. Tabor Philoteria Yarmuk River

Dora Exaloth Emmatha Abila

Nain Aendor Gadara

Legio Iezrael

Maximianopolis Agrippina

Caesarea (Capercotnei) Scythopolis

Taanach Pella

Narbata Ginae

Salumias

Abelmea

Sebaste Gerasa
(Samaria)

Apollonia Neapolis

Sychar Jabbok River

Yarkon River Acrabbein Coreae

Joppa Antipatris Alexandrium
Pegae (Sartaba)

Onus Timnah Phasaelis Gadora

Lydda Aramatha Aphairema

Jamnia Modin Gophna Archelais

Machmas Ephrajm Philadelphia

Emmaus Jericho Livias

Accaron Cyprus Esbus

Azotus Jerusalem Bethany

Bethther Qumran Medeba

Ascalon Bethlehem Hyrcania

Betogabris Adollam Beth Herodium
zechariah

Anthedon Tricomias Macherus

Gaza Hebron

Adora

Sycomazon Thella Duma Chermela Dead Sea

Menois Orda Asthemoe Arnon River

Raphia Eremmon Anea

Birsama Iethira Masada

Beersheba

Elusa

Thamara

Mampsis Zoar Zered River

Eboda

Jordan River

feet	m
8202	2500
6561	2000
4921	1500
3280	1000
1640	500
820	250
0	0

Below sea level

0 10 20 30 40 miles

0 20 40 60 km

Column from Codex Sinaiticus

17

© carta

CHRONOLOGICAL TABLE

Column group 1: Mesopotamia | Palestine | Egypt | West

Date	Mesopotamia	Palestine	Egypt	West
2300	Sargon I, Naram-Sin (Kingdom of Akkad)		6th Dynasty	Early Kingdom
2200		Rise in Population		
2100	3rd Dynasty of Ur, Gudea of Lagash, Independent Assyria		1st Intermediate Period	
2000		Amorite Wave		Middle Kingdom
1900			12th Dynasty	
1800	Mari Period, Hammurabi		2nd Intermediate Period (13th Dynasty)	
1700			Hyksos Rule (16th-17th Dynasties)	
1600	Cassite Dynasty in Babylon			
1500		Strengthening of Egyptian Control	18th Dynasty	New Kingdom
1400		El-Amarna Period		Downfall of Crete; Height of Mycenaean Culture
1300		Strengthening of Egyptian control	19th Dynasty	
1200	Minor Kingdoms	Israelite Wave of Conquest; Philistine Penetration	Syrian Interregnum	Achaian Invasion of Greece; Trojan war
1100		Institution of Kingship in Israel	20th Dynasty	
1000		Divided Monarchy	21st Dynasty	Dorian Invasion of Greece
900	Assyrian Empire		22nd Dynasty	Etruscan Invasion of Italy; Homer; First Olympic Games
800		Destruction of Samaria and Exile of Israel	23rd-25th Dynasties	
700		Destruction of Jerusalem and Exile of Judah	Assyrian Conquest; 26th Dynasty	Height of Etruscan Culture
600	Babylonian Empire	Restoration of Zion	Persian Conquest	Roman Republic Established; Persian Wars; Herodotus; Decline of Athens
500	Persian Empire		28th-30th Dynasties	
400	Conquest of Alexander the Great			
300	Seleucid Rule	Ptolemaic Rule	Ptolemaic Rule	Punic Wars; Hannibal
200	Parthian Empire	Seleucid Rule; Maccabeans		Roman Rule in Greece
100		King Herod; Birth of Jesus		Caesar
B.C./A.D.		Destruction of Second Temple	Roman Rule	Roman Empire
100	Parthian Wars			

Column group 2: Palestine — Judea | Israel (Period of the Judges / Period of Israelite Settlement)

Date	Judea	Israel
1260	Period of Israelite Conquest	
1200	Deborah's War	
1160	Philistine Penetration	
1060	Battle of Aphek	
1040	Samuel	
1020	Saul	
980	David	
940	Solomon	
920	Rehoboam	Jeroboam son of Nebat
900	Asa	Baasha
860	Jehoshaphat	Ahab
840	Elisha; Jehoash	Jehu
820	Jonah; Jehoash	
800	Amos; Amaziah	

(Side labels: Elijah, Elisha, Jonah, Amos — Period of the Judges / Period of Israelite Settlement)

Column group 3: Palestine — Judea | Israel (Assyrian Province / Babylonian Province / Persian Satrapies)

Date	Judea	Israel
780	Uzziah	Jeroboam II
740	Ahaz	Menahem; Pekah; Hoshea; Fall of Samaria
700	Hezekiah	Assyrian Province
620	Josiah	
600		Egyptian Rule
580	Destruction of Temple	Babylonian Province
460	Ezra	
440	Nehemiah	
340	Conquered by Alexander	
320	Overrun by Antigonus; Overrun by Ptolemy I	Wars of Diadochi

(Side labels: Hosea, Isaiah, Micah, Zephaniah, Jeremiah, Habakkuk, Obadiah, Ezekiel, Deutero-Isaiah, Haggai, Zechariah, Malachi — Persian Satrapies)

Column group 4: Palestine (Ptolemaic / Seleucid / Maccabean / Roman Rule)

Date	Palestine
300	Simon son of Onias, High Priest
240	Onias II son of Simon, High Priest
220	Battle of Raphia
200	Battle of Panias; Conquest of Antiochus III
180	Onias III High Priest
160	Maccabean Revolt; Death of Judas Maccabeus
140	Jonathan High Priest; Simon High Priest
120	John High Priest
100	Judas High Priest
80	Civil War; Janneus; Hyrcanus II High Priest; Siege of Pompey
40	Parthian Invasion
20	Reign of Herod
B.C.	Birth of Jesus; Archelaus
A.D.	
20	Philip Antipas; Jesus' Ministry
40	Agrippa I King of Judea
60	Ministry of Apostles; First Jewish Revolt; Destruction of Jerusalem; Fall of Masada
80	Jewish Center at Jamnia
140	Bar Kokhba Revolt; Fall of Bethther
160	Spread of Christianity

(Side labels: Ptolemaic Rule, Seleucid Rule, Maccabean Rule, First Procurators, Agrippa II Later Procurators, Roman Rule)